PREPARING FOR GAME DAY

CHEERLEADING
Techniques For Performing

PREPARING FOR GAME DAY

BASEBALL & SOFTBALL: SUCCESS ON THE DIAMOND

BASKETBALL: STRATEGY ON THE HARDWOOD

CHEERLEADING: TECHNIQUES FOR PERFORMING

EXTREME SPORTS: POINTERS FOR PUSHING THE LIMITS

FOOTBALL: TOUGHNESS ON THE GRIDIRON

LACROSSE: FACING OFF ON THE FIELD

SOCCER: BREAKING AWAY ON THE PITCH

TRACK & FIELD: CONDITIONING FOR GREATNESS

VOLLEYBALL: APPROACHING THE NET

WRESTLING: CONTENDING ON THE MAT

PREPARING FOR GAME DAY

CHEERLEADING
Techniques For Performing

Peter Douglas

MASON CREST

Mason Crest
450 Parkway Drive, Suite D
Broomall, Pennsylvania 19008
(866) MCP-BOOK (toll free)

First printing
9 8 7 6 5 4 3 2 1

ISBN (hardback) 978-1-4222-3915-5
ISBN (series) 978-1-4222-3912-4
ISBN (ebook) 978-1-4222-7870-3

Cataloging-in-Publication Data on file with the Library of Congress

QR CODES AND LINKS TO THIRD-PARTY CONTENT

CONTENTS

KEY ICONS TO LOOK FOR:

Words to understand: These words with their easy-to-understand definitions will increase the reader's understanding of the text while building vocabulary skills.

Sidebars: This boxed material within the main text allows readers to build knowledge, gain insights, explore possibilities, and broaden their perspectives by weaving together additional information to provide realistic and holistic perspectives.

Educational Videos: Readers can view videos by scanning our QR codes, providing them with additional educational content to supplement the text. Examples include news coverage, moments in history, speeches, iconic sports moments and much more!

Text-dependent questions: These questions send the reader back to the text for more careful attention to the evidence presented there.

Research projects: Readers are pointed toward areas of further inquiry connected to each chapter. Suggestions are provided for projects that encourage deeper research and analysis.

Series glossary of key terms: This back-of-the book glossary contains terminology used throughout this series. Words found here increase the reader's ability to read and comprehend higher-level books and articles in this field.

 WORDS TO UNDERSTAND:

choreography: the sequence of steps and movements in dance or figure skating, especially in a ballet or other staged dance

conducive: making a certain situation or outcome likely or possible

venue: the place where an event takes place

Chapter 1

COMPETITION DAY

The better prepared an athlete is when it comes time to compete, the better the chance of a successful result. This is true in any sport, and cheerleading is no different. Competitive cheerleading is a physically challenging activity, and athletes need to take preparation seriously if they want to perform at their best.

> 66 To go out there that one time, knowing that this is it, this is what counts, the pressure's on, and to be able to nail it, that just says a lot. I think that entails the motivation for all of them. 99

– Jomo Thompson, twelve-time UCA national champion head coach, University of Kentucky Wildcats

THE NIGHT BEFORE

The first steps to a great competition day are taken the night before. Especially if you are leaving for the competition **venue** in the morning, it is a good idea to get everything you will need together and ready to go before you go to bed the night before. This way, you will have one less thing to think or worry about when it is time to get ready to leave.

Take the time to check your uniform and equipment. Are all components of your

It is a good idea to check and prepare any equipment needed the night before a competition.

uniform pieces accounted for and clean? Check for snags, rips, or stains. Make sure buttons are secure and zippers are working properly. Check for any pins that may have been put in previously. Write yourself a checklist to help ensure nothing is forgotten. Examples might include: megaphones, vest and top (bodyliner), signs, skirt and/or shorts, pom-poms, socks, water bottles, shoes, hair bows, and briefs. Double-check everything so that you are not second-guessing if you have remembered everything in the morning, including extras of any items that may come in handy, like socks or briefs.

Another tip for the night before comes in handy if you are on the road in an unfamiliar city for your competition. It is a good idea to plan your route to the venue ahead of time. Global positioning system (GPS) navigation is a great thing, but it is not perfect. Punch in

> *"We talk to the freshmen and we make sure it's known in their hearts and in their minds that they put 110 percent out there no matter what the situation. We make sure that they do their best each and every time."*
>
> *– Alli Greer, three-time UCA national college champion*

GPS navigation is generally reliable but not perfect. Double-check your route to the venue the night before.

the details into your GPS, and make sure the destination it brings up makes sense. Pull up a map online to double-check if you have any doubt about the location it is showing. You never know when traffic, weather, or other factors will slow down your commute, so plan your route with these factors in mind. Your GPS device can help you avoid traffic and construction, but this will add time to your trip. If you are at a hotel, ask at the front desk how long it will take to get to the venue in the morning and if there are any construction concerns along the route. Again, getting this squared away the night before will eliminate last-minute scrambling and the stress of rushing to be on time.

Once all your gear is assembled and packed up, go to bed. The night before a competition is not the night to invite members from the squad for a sleepover. Try your best to get to sleep at a reasonable hour. According to the National Sleep Foundation, people age fourteen to twenty-five should ideally get eight or nine hours of sleep to function at their best. Keep that target in mind while getting ready the night before, and give yourself plenty of time to get a good night's sleep. Not sleeping well can significantly affect an athlete's performance as well as mood and ability to focus. Do not put yourself in that position; make getting good rest a priority.

> "(When practicing) you need to be in the presence of a qualified coach, and you also need to be sure that you're on the right type of padded surface."
>
> – Linda Gooch, two-time national champion head coach, University of Central Florida

> " More than anything we trust each other. We trust each other, we trust the bases, the flyers, the backspots, to all collectively do their job, and because we trust each other, it comes out on the mat. "
>
> – Clark Kelly, 2015 UCA national college champion

EAT BREAKFAST

In all your pre-event planning, an important step is to make sure you leave yourself enough time to eat a healthy breakfast. Feeling nervous or not feeling hungry are excuses that need to be overcome, so you can fuel your body properly for the competition. If you need to force yourself to eat, then that is what you should do. Be in charge of your own nutrition rather than letting your hunger dictate when, and sometimes what, you eat. Snack bars and concession stands are not renowned for their healthy food options. So be sure to eat well in the morning and put your body in the best possible position to perform well.

Breakfast on competition day should include a balance of carbohydrates and protein, such as Greek yogurt, fruit, and peanut butter on toast with low-fat milk for a morning competition. If you are competing in the afternoon, make your breakfast a little heartier by adding two eggs or two turkey sausage links.

If the competition is in the evening, then you should eat the hearty breakfast and add another serving of carbohydrates,

"The back girl is always counting. The back person in a stunt should control the stunt. Make sure you have a nice deep pocket on a thigh stand. The backspot also catches the waist as it comes down."

– Brandy Corcoran, NCAA Division II and NAIA national champion coach

Greek yogurt with fruit provides a good balance of protein and carbs for cheerleaders on competition mornings.

10

like a bowl of oatmeal. Then eat a significant lunch at about midday. This should consist of a serving of vegetables, carbohydrates from fruit, and a serving of protein, such as a grilled chicken breast.

About thirty minutes before heading to warm-ups, all competitors should eat a small snack, like an apple and a banana. This will help top up your energy tank for when it is time to hit the floor and compete.

> 66 Think about all the good things that you've done when you've stunted. Don't just let one fall take over, because that's fear. As long as you know what you are doing and you have done it a lot, it should be second nature to you. 99
>
> – Gabi Butler, two-time All Star national champion

After the competition is over, that is no reason to abandon good nutrition. Finish the day by eating a smart dinner. Here is an example:

- one serving of protein (chicken breast, steak, salmon, etc.)

- one serving of complex or nutrient-dense carbs (brown rice, chili, a scoop of mashed potatoes, etc.)

- one serving of vegetables (a salad would be perfect, but go easy on the dressing)

Throughout the entire day, do not forget to keep hydrated. Given that energy is being expended in widely spaced, two-and-a-half-minute segments, water is the only drink you will need. Sports drinks are popular but contain additional empty calories that cheer athletes do not need, especially because they are not losing excessive nutrients through sweating.

Try to drink at east twenty ounces (590 ml) of water the morning of the competition. If you are competing later in the day, drink an additional eight ounces (240 ml) at least thirty minutes before your warm-ups. Otherwise, drink as your thirst dictates throughout the day. Hydration is important to keep up your energy and strength, but it has an added benefit for cheerleaders as well. Water can help during the cheer portion of your routine by keeping your vocal cords lubricated and helping you avoid dry mouth, so remember to pack a couple of bottles in your cheer bag.

STRETCH YOUR MUSCLES

Before you head out for warm-ups, it is crucial to make sure you stretch properly first. Proper stretching is the most effective thing you can do to help reduce the risk of getting injured. Cheerleading is a full-body activity, so stretching should be comprehensive of all your muscle groups. Spend between fifteen and thirty minutes stretching, making sure to hold each stretch for twenty to thirty seconds. Here are some examples of stretching routines that will prepare your muscles and get them loose for the competition.

Stretching before a competition helps give muscles flexibility like that displayed by this University of Maryland cheerleader.

- Chest and Shoulder Stretch: Clasp your hands behind your back, and raise your arms as high as you can to stretch your shoulders and chest.

- Triceps Stretch: Stretch the back of your arm by reaching one hand up and behind your head to touch the center of your back, while you grasp that elbow with your opposite hand. Pull downward to feel the stretch.

- Back and Shoulder Stretch: Reach one arm in front of your body and across your chest; grasp that arm above the elbow with your opposite hand, and pull toward your body.

- Quad Stretch: Bend one knee backward, and grab that ankle with the hand on the same side; balance yourself and pull your ankle toward your body.

- Hip Stretch: Spread your legs wide with your feet pointing outward. Next, squat down and balance your elbows on your knees, stretching your hips as you squat as far as you can.

- Hamstring Stretch: Sit on the ground, and spread your legs wide. Reach to one side, and grasp your ankle with one or both hands, depending on your flexibility.

- Abs and Back: Lie on your stomach, and place your palms on the floor just wider than your shoulders. Press up and lift your torso from the ground as you arch your back.

> *"I'm a flyer, which requires a lot of flexibility and confidence in the air. You have to have a lot of body control and awareness to know what you're doing. I don't get scared—I just go for it. I really trust my teammates."*
>
> *– Carly Manning, five-time NCA national champion and three-time world champion*

13

This is just a sample stretching routine. Your coach may have a specific routine and order that he or she wants you to follow. If a stretch does not feel good or causes pain, do not push it. Back off immediately, and find an alternate way to stretch that muscle.

WARM UP

Once you are properly stretched out, it is time to warm up the rest of the body. An active warm-up will get your blood flowing and keep those muscles supple and loose. Cheerleading involves a lot of dynamic movements using all muscle groups. A good warm-up should address every area of the body. A light jog is a great place to start. Running in place will do if the venue or weather is not **conducive** to a jog. After about five to seven minutes of jogging, there are several options to get and keep the body warm:

- Jumping jacks

- Sliding from side to side

- Bounding or skipping exercises

- Jogging backward

- Doing the grapevine by crossing one foot in front of the other

Cheerleaders warm up backstage at a competition in Russia.

Spend about forty-five seconds to a minute on each of these until you have broken a light sweat and feel properly loosened up.

Watch a routine from 2017 NCA All Star national champions Top Gun from Miami.

GET FOCUSED

Now it is almost time to compete. You have put in all the work. You know your **choreography** in your sleep. You are rested, nourished, and ready to go physically. This is the time when everything changes. In practice and preparation, performing well is 90 percent physical and 10 percent mental. When it comes time to perform, the reverse is often true. Your technique, conditioning, and routine preparation have all brought you to this point. Now, you have to find what it takes to stay focused and concentrate. You have to be confident in your preparation and your ability to execute. Block out thoughts of past mistakes, thinking only of the dozens of other times you have performed that section of the routine flawlessly.

Train yourself to be mentally tough, pushing all negativity and self-doubt aside. A successful athlete has no time for either of those things. Do not put yourself in situations to psych yourself out. For example, do not

"I make a schedule because that helps me stay focused with everything I have going on. Mentally, I go through the routine in my head so that I just nail it on the stage.

– Dee Temples, 2014 Superstar of All Stars

15

"In both competitive and sideline cheerleading, individual success is dependent on the success of the group and their ability to work together."

– Peyton Mabry, three-time NCA National Champion and 2012 world champion

watch other teams perform their routines. If they execute stronger stunts or tougher tumbling than you have in your routine, there is no advantage in having that knowledge. It is too late to change your routine, so being put in a place to be thinking that your routine is inferior is just a distraction that hurts your concentration. Think positive, and focus solely on nailing your own routine.

Practice clearing your mind and finding your center. There are a lot of distractions going on backstage at a competition. Train yourself to block those things out, so you can have laser focus for two and a half minutes. This is something you can practice, just like any other part of your routine. As the saying goes, the mind is the athlete's strongest muscle, and it can be strengthened and exercised with practice. The more you practice clearing your mind of distractions, the easier it will be to do when it comes time to step on that mat and compete.

Here is an example of a ritual you could use to get in the zone right before competing:

1) Breathing: Inhale confidence and exhale stress. Do this several times.

2) Self-Talk: Create a trigger statement that tells you that you are ready for competition. Try something like "game on" or "let's do this." Make it personal and meaningful to you.

3) Body Language: Use an action like clapping your hands or shaking it off to signal you are ready to shift 100 percent into focus. Then walk out and step onto the mat with a confident stride.

TEXT-DEPENDENT QUESTIONS:

1. According to the National Sleep Foundation, people age fourteen to twenty-five should ideally get how many hours of sleep to function at their best?

2. Explain how an athlete might stretch his or her quad.

3. Give an example of how you might put yourself in a situation to psych yourself out before competing.

 # RESEARCH PROJECT:

Take some time, and put together a pre-competition routine for yourself. Write it out, being detailed in each element, outlining specific warm-up exercises or drills. Make the routine specific to whether you are a backspot, base, or flyer. Outline meals, rest, and all the necessary components that you feel could help best prepare you before a big competition.

WORDS TO UNDERSTAND:

affirmations: positively worded statements that reflect a desire or goal

endeavor: activity directed toward a goal

perspective: the ability to understand what is important and what isn't

Chapter 2

THE RIGHT MIND-SET

Good preparation is the best prevention when it comes to sports injuries. This is no different for cheerleading, an activity that combines gymnastics, dance, and tumbling. Cheerleading takes place on a variety of surfaces, including asphalt, polished wood, and grass. It's important to be warmed up and prepared for whatever comes your way.

Cheerleading can contain risky maneuvers, so it is important to be mentally focused and concentrating well.

For an athletic **endeavor** like cheerleading, obviously the body needs to be prepared to compete. Often overlooked, however, is that so does the mind. For a long time, many people in the Western world believed that the mind and the body were two completely separate things. However, we are now coming to understand more and more about the connections between the body and the mind. In fact, they are not separate at all; what you think and feel correlate directly to your physical state. In turn, how your body feels affects the types of messages sent to the brain, affecting your mental state.

Make use of that physical-to-mental connection during your preparations. If you are injured or too tired to continue, don't ignore your feelings;

take a break. If you feel thirsty, be sure to stay hydrated to avoid problems later on. Taking hints from your body can improve your performance drastically, so don't ignore what it's telling you.

Skill and technique are important, but so too are concentration, awareness, and discipline. Mental preparation that builds these qualities can take many forms, including imagery, goal setting and attitude, developing a sense of humor, and positive thinking.

IMAGERY

Imagery in terms of sports preparation means you see yourself in your mind's eye performing an activity correctly and without injury. Suppose, for example, you are concerned about a new cheerleading routine you need to master. Close your eyes, and picture yourself in your head performing the routine perfectly. When it comes time to actually do the routine, the fact that you have rehearsed it mentally so many times will give you the confidence to perform without making mistakes.

AIM HIGH

It is important to set achievable goals at the beginning of any endeavor, athletic or otherwise. Personal goals, goals you have as a cheerleading

Writing down goals helps make them more real and will provide focus as you plan the steps to reach them.

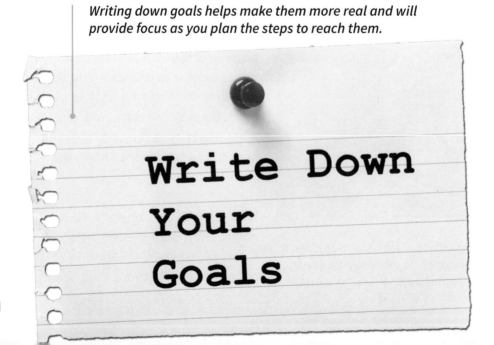

team, or a combination of both can help you stay focused and motivated. Think about what it is you want to achieve as a cheerleader, and keep in mind that no goal is too big or too small. Your goals could include mastering a difficult jump, learning a new dance routine, or making a particular cheerleading team.

Do not rely on committing your goals to memory. Be sure to write them down. The act of writing down your goals will make them more concrete in your mind and can also serve as a constant reminder of what you are trying to achieve. Put your list of goals in a place where you will look at them at least a couple times a day, such as your bathroom mirror or your locker at school.

> " I make a list for myself of what I want to achieve. Then I bring it to my coach and see what he thinks would be the best skills for me to learn at that time.
>
> – Kiara Nowlin, three-time USASF All Star world champion "

GET INSPIRED

Setting goals is one thing. Sticking to the pursuit of them is quite another. It is easy to let the temptation to quit creep in. Combat these feelings by looking for inspiration. When you feel inspired, you have an attitude in which you believe you can do anything you set your mind to—and you can! Inspire yourself by finding quotations or sayings you find meaningful, watch performances by an accomplished cheerleader you admire, or even have a pep talk with your coach or fellow teammate. Also, write down sayings that inspire you, and leave them where you can read the quotes often, near your written-down goals. By reminding yourself what your goals are, why you have them, and visualizing yourself achieving those things, you will go a long way toward mastering them.

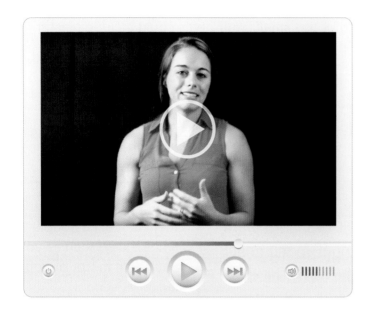

Registered dietician and former college competitive cheerleader Nicole Aucoin offers tips on what to eat before a workout.

Positive thinking and affirmations are two of the techniques cheerleaders can use to improve their mental preparation.

POSITIVELY STATED

Affirmations are another good way to get yourself mentally prepared for cheerleading. These are positively worded statements that reflect a desire or goal. For example, you could repeat this sentence to yourself over and over: "I am doing my absolute best, and I am good!"

If you find yourself in a situation that makes you nervous, like cheer tryouts, there could be several factors for your anxiety. There are cheers to memorize, routines to learn, and you have to come up with your own routine and perform it in front of many people—possibly even the whole school!

You could always panic, but it would be more helpful to try this technique: close your eyes and visualize yourself performing the cheer or routine correctly. Let your imagination run free. Imagine that everyone is clapping and cheering for you because you did such a great job. Picture yourself in the cheerleading uniform at the big football game, leading the crowds in cheers of victory. Repeat affirmations to yourself, such as, "I am a member of the cheerleading squad," or, "I am performing my routines perfectly."

These kinds of affirmations should be said as if you are doing them right now, as opposed to sometime in the future. By phrasing your affirmations this way, the goals are made more concrete and real in your mind. There's an old adage that says, "Fake it 'til you make it." By pretending you are a successful cheerleader and imagining yourself as such, it may not be long before your dream becomes a reality!

HAVE A SENSE OF HUMOR

Of course, despite affirmations, imagery, inspirational sayings, and other positive approaches, there will still be setbacks. Disappointment is only natural, especially if you don't make the squad you'd hoped or you make a mistake in front of the crowd, but when these things happen, keep them in **perspective**, and maintain a sense of humor. Things could always be worse.

In disappointment or even embarrassment, a sense of humor will help you do better in cheerleading—as well as in life. Often, being able to laugh at yourself helps you stay focused and motivated. If you take yourself too seriously, you can easily become flustered and make even more mistakes.

Spirit Curse

Cheerleading camps use spirit sticks (usually a wooden dowel painted red, white, and blue) as a symbol of cheerleading's essence. Following a tradition started by Lawrence Herkimer, at the end of camp, the spirit stick is presented to the team that best demonstrates teamwork and a spirit of support for all the other teams. This award is not about skill, execution, or technique. It is all about attitude. The stick-giving tradition has spread from camps to individual squads, who will often award a spirit stick of their own to individual members that demonstrate the best attitude. Sticks are either passed down from squad to squad each year, or each year's squad will create their own stick for the season. Once you receive a spirit stick, however, many cheerleaders believe that you need to be very careful with it.

The superstition of the spirit stick is that if you drop it, your season will be cursed. The length of that curse varies depending on which version of the superstition is being followed. Some believe dropping the spirit stick will curse a cheerleader's entire cheer career.

STEP ON A CRACK . . .

Other sports are well-known for the superstitious nature of their athletes, but superstitions are uncommon in cheerleading. Few cheerleaders care about wearing a certain pair of socks or an item of clothing the way baseball players do—but cheerleading is known for the spirit stick, a type of baton used at cheerleading camps. It is awarded not to the squad that is necessarily the best technically but to the one that possesses the best sportsmanship, team spirit, and overall inspiring, positive energy.

Despite the lack of a basis in fact, superstitions can inspire and build confidence and therefore can be an effective tool for mental preparation for cheerleading. By the same token, however, a broken superstition can have the opposite effect.

The spirit stick is the one truly superstitious object in cheerleading. If dropped, some believe that the responsible cheerleader and the team will be cursed.

TEXT-DEPENDENT QUESTIONS:

1. Besides skill and technique, name three additional elements that are important for success.

2. Where can you find inspiration to stay positive and motivated?

3. Give an example of an affirmation.

 RESEARCH PROJECT:

Plan and choreograph a stunt of your own design. Write out the specific steps for backspots, bases, and flyers, including how many of each would be required. Be detailed!

WORDS TO UNDERSTAND:

clasp: a holding or enveloping with the hands or arms

crucial: very important

inclement: (regarding weather) unpleasantly cold or wet

Chapter 3

TRAINING FOR SUCCESS

Safety should always be of primary concern when preparing for a physically demanding sport like cheerleading. Cheerleaders are often required to perform movements such as jumps, splits, and other gymnastics routines. If the athletes are not warmed up properly, these routines could lead to serious injury. In this chapter, a sample of stretches from head to toe is explained to ensure safe performance.

Here are some tips about stretching:

- Each stretch should be held for a minimum of ten seconds. You can increase your flexibility by holding the stretches for longer periods of time—twenty to thirty seconds—and performing them more often.

- Do not bounce or jerk your muscles when you are stretching. This can tear or strain muscles.

- Do not rush through your stretches simply to be done with them. This does your body no good and will often lead to injury. Always make sure to take the time to warm up properly.

- Listen to your body, and respect its limits. A small amount of discomfort is expected when stretching, but if something causes you excessive pain, stop immediately. Do not compare your stretching ability to anyone else's; everyone has his or her own particular abilities.

> *What you really want to think about when you are doing body positions (during workouts) is not just the flexibility part of it, but the muscle part. You really have to work on every single part of your body, but your core is what holds everything together."*
>
> *– Sarah Swicegood,*
> *Cheer Legend coach*

Pulling the head gently toward the shoulder can enhance side-to-side neck stretches.

NECK STRETCHES

1. Side-to-Side Stretch: Stand with your legs shoulder width apart. Tuck your chin into your chest, and hold for ten to twenty seconds. Tilt your right ear toward your right shoulder, and hold for ten to twenty seconds. Return to the center. Tilt the left ear toward the left shoulder, and again hold for ten to twenty seconds. Repeat three times on each side.

2. Rotational Stretch: Stand with your feet shoulder width apart. Slowly rotate your head to the right, and look over your right shoulder until you feel a gentle stretch. Hold for ten to twenty seconds. Bring the head to face forward again, and then rotate the neck to the left, looking over the left shoulder until you feel a gentle stretch. Hold for ten to twenty seconds.

SHOULDER AND ARM STRETCHES

The arm and shoulder muscles are heavily used in cheerleading. Here are some effective ways to keep them loose.

1. Stand with your feet shoulder width apart. **Clasp** your hands behind your back with your elbows fully extended. Then raise your arms as high as you can until you feel a gentle stretch. Hold for ten to twenty seconds.

2. Stand with your feet shoulder width apart. Raise both arms above your head, and bend the left elbow, then grasp it with the right hand. Pull your left upper arm gently toward the middle of your body. You should feel this stretch in your triceps muscle. Hold for ten to twenty seconds.

3. Raise your arms above your head again, then bend the right elbow, and grasp it with your left hand. Pull your right upper arm gently toward the middle of your body until you feel a gentle stretch in your triceps. Hold for ten to twenty seconds.

4. Stand with your feet shoulder width apart. Clasp your hands behind your back, with your elbows fully extended. Lift your arms slightly, and bend over at the waist, then lift your arms up even farther, if you can, and hold this stretch for ten to twenty seconds. Repeat two more times.

5. To work both the arms and the waist, stand with your feet shoulder width apart. Clasp your hands over your head, with your elbows straight. Bend at the waist, and lean to the left until you feel a gentle stretch. Hold for ten to twenty seconds. Return to the starting position, then bend at the waist, and lean to the right, again holding for ten to twenty seconds.

A triceps stretch is one of several for the arm and shoulders that cheerleaders should do before workouts.

Stretching and flexibility are crucial for cheerleaders, but despite routines being just two and a half minutes long, strength and conditioning come into play as well. Here are some tips to follow from livestrong.com:

Building Endurance

To perform for two and a half minutes straight, competitive cheerleaders need endurance. Cardiovascular exercise is what will build endurance. A great way to train for endurance at practice is to perform three to five repetitions of your competition routine in sequence. Running is another cardiovascular activity that can easily be done by the entire squad at practice. Outside of practice, cheerleaders should be encouraged to participate in aerobic activities such as rollerblading, biking, or aerobic dance classes. At least half of your daily training time should be devoted to increasing cardiovascular endurance.

Strength Training

Lifting other cheerleaders in stunts and holding your own body weight in tumbling require a great deal of strength. When strength training as a squad, a good option is body weight exercises such as push-ups and sit-ups because they do not require any equipment to be shared by your entire squad. For independent training, lifting weights is a great option. Cheerleaders should be trained in proper form and should always lift weights with a spotting partner. Strength training should be done at least three days per week.

Better Balance

Balance is important not just for the top person in stunts. Bases need good balance as well, and tumbling and jumps require steady balance too. Standing balance poses from yoga are a great way to balance train. Put a cheerleading spin on your poses by making them mimic stunting positions. For example, instead of doing the tree pose from yoga, turn it into a Liberty with your arms above your head in a high V motion. Incorporate at least one balance exercise into your training routine every day. Hold balance poses for thirty seconds or longer, breathing deeply throughout them. As you progress you may want to train on a balance cushion or pillow that will challenge your stability even more.

LEG AND ANKLE STRETCHES

Be sure to take time to properly stretch your legs. It is all too easy for cheerleaders to pull or strain a muscle—even tear it—by performing high kicks, jumps, or splits before their legs are properly warmed up. Use the following exercises as a guide.

1. Hamstrings: Sit on the floor with your legs stretched straight out in front of you. Your feet should be about hip width apart. Keep your legs as straight as possible, then reach forward and grab hold of either your ankles or toes, depending on your level of flexibility. Hold for ten to twenty seconds. You should feel this stretch in the backs of the knees and your lower back. Try it with your toes pointing straight up and with your toes pointing forward.

2. Groin: Sit on the floor with your knees bent and the soles of your feet pressed together. Hold your feet with your hands, and then rest your elbows on your lower legs. Lean forward, and try to touch your forehead to the floor while you press down on your legs. Hold for ten to twenty seconds.

3. Calves: Stand facing a wall, and place your hands at about shoulder height. Place one foot in front of the other, keeping the heel of your back foot firmly on the floor. Place your weight on your forward, bent leg, and lean forward, as if you are trying to push against the wall. Hold for ten to twenty seconds. Repeat for the other leg.

4. Calves: You need a flight of stairs or a sturdy box. First, line up your heels with the edge of the step. Then move your feet back so that the balls of your feet are on the edge of the step and your heels hang off the edge. (You may need to lean against something or hold on to a railing for balance.) Slowly dip your heels down, and then come back up. Repeat ten times.

If running is part of your fitness routine, be sure to stretch out your calves before hitting the pavement.

5. Ankles: Stand with your legs shoulder width apart. Point your right toe so that it is touching the ground, and roll your ankle in a clockwise direction three times. Then roll the ankle counterclockwise three times. Repeat with the left foot.

Check out these stretching tips for cheerleaders from world champion All Star cheerleader Gabi Butler.

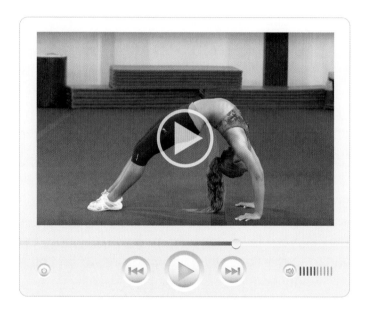

CHEERLEADING SPECIFIC EXERCISES

Cheerleaders often perform moves that involve jumps, splits, and tumbling as well as partner stunts or pyramids. Here are a few additional exercises you can do to build strength in particular areas.

HAMSTRINGS

Sit with your legs spread wide apart. Lean over your left leg, and grab hold of the toes of your left foot or left ankle. Point your toes forward, and hold for ten to twenty seconds. Sit up. Turn so that you are facing the center, and then lean over your right leg, grabbing hold of the toes of your right foot or ankle. Point your toes forward and hold for ten to twenty seconds. Sit up.

Stretching the hamstrings helps maintain flexibility in the legs.

Turn so that you are facing the center, and then lean over your right leg, grabbing hold of the toes of your right foot or ankle. Point your toes forward, and hold for ten to twenty seconds.

ABS, LEGS, AND ARMS

Strong abdominals, legs, and arms are the keys to being able to perform jumps effectively and without injury. You can strengthen these areas by performing the following exercises:

1. Push-Ups: Start in a facedown position on the floor. Your back should be level, your toes should be on the floor, and your arms should be locked with your hands shoulder width apart. To vary this exercise, try moving your arms farther out away from the shoulders (about six to nine inches [fifteen to twenty-three centimeters) or closer to the body (about four inches [ten centimeters]).

2. T Jumps: Start in a standing position, feet slightly apart. Jump up into the air, bringing your knees as high as possible to the front of your body. Slap your shins when you have reached the highest point in your jump. Extend your arms into a T shape when you land. Repeat this five times, working up to ten repetitions.

Push-ups are an effective resistance exercise for building upper body strength.

3. V Sit: Sit on the floor. Lie down on your back with your arms extended along your sides. Your legs should be stretched out straight. Raise your legs at least two inches (five centimeters) off the floor, with your toes pointed. At the same time, lift your upper body halfway up. You should be looking something like the letter V. Hold for ten to twenty seconds. Lower your body and legs, but do not let anything touch the floor. Repeat five to ten times.

Ankle injuries are a leading cause of discomfort and loss of participation time among cheerleaders. The following exercise can help you strengthen your ankles:

Sit on the floor with your legs straight. Using a mini resistance band, place the band around both feet at the base of your toes. Keep one foot firmly in place, and use the other to pull the band outward and upward while rotating the foot. Hold for ten to twenty seconds. Return to the starting position as slowly as possible, then repeat with the other leg. Repeat this exercise for five to ten minutes a day, working up to twenty minutes.

With all the stress they endure from tumbling and partner stunts, it is **crucial** to have strong wrists. The following two exercises work to help develop your wrist muscles.

1. Using a light dumbbell weighing one to three pounds (half to one and a half kilograms), sit in a chair with your knees bent at a ninety-degree angle. Hold the weight with your palm facing down and with your forearm on your thigh. Slowly bend your wrist upward as far as possible. Hold this position for ten seconds, and then lower the wrist slowly, keeping your forearm on your thigh. Repeat ten times.

Wrist curls with dumbbells help to build strength in the wrists. The stronger a joint is, the better it can withstand injury.

2. Seated in a chair with your knees bent, position the dumbbell as in the previous exercise. This time, your hand should be facing palm up. Slowly bend the wrist as far as possible, holding for ten seconds, then lowering slowly. Repeat ten times.

CHEER GEAR

Cheerleaders, like any other athlete, should stretch and warm up before workouts, practice, or competitions. Despite the danger of falls, cheerleaders do not wear safety equipment.

There are, however, types of equipment commonly associated with cheerleaders: megaphones, pom-poms, and various types of signs as well as the ever-present cheerleading uniform, which is worn with pride. Although none of this equipment offers safety or protection, some thought should be given to the design of the uniform itself, which may help to prevent certain injuries from occurring.

In cold-weather conditions, cheerleaders' uniforms include pants and heavy jackets.

There is quite a bit of variation in cheerleading uniforms. Different teams will mix and match a sweater, sweatshirt, skirt, vest, top, pants, or shorts. All are in school or team colors with a logo or design. Many schools have two or even three different types of uniforms. Which uniform is worn depends on several factors, including whether the sport is conducted inside or outside and what the weather is like. For example, football games, especially in high school and college, are played outdoors and in a season where there can be **inclement** weather.

For a cold-weather sport like football, cheerleading uniforms consist of skirts or pants and a sweater, all in heavy material such as wool or a polyester blend. Sometimes, heavy jackets and gloves are worn if the weather is especially severe.

Things are different at a basketball game in an indoor gymnasium that is often warm, thanks to all the fans, cheerleaders, and players packed into it. In this case, cheerleading uniforms might consist of a skirt, pants, and a short-sleeved shirt or vest. These items are made out of fabric that is lighter in weight, such as cotton or a rayon blend.

The most important part of the cheerleader's uniform is the shoes. Always purchase a shoe that provides you with the maximum amount of support and comfort. Remember, ankle injuries are some of the most common injuries sustained by cheerleaders. Canvas or flat-soled shoes (i.e., with no shaping at all on the sole) should not be worn because they offer no support for the ankles or arches, which can lead to a twisted ankle, shin splints, or worse.

Many cheerleading supply or uniform stores offer specific cheerleading shoes, or you can find them online. Take the time to make sure the shoe fits properly. Such shoes can be expensive, but they are well worth the cost. There may be an outlet store in your area that sells well-trusted brand names at discount prices.

Inserts may also be used to give shoes maximum comfort and support. These are special pads that go into the shoe and help prevent pressure on a specific part of the foot or prevent abnormal movement of the foot. They can be purchased in grocery stores, department stores, and specialty shoe stores. Talk to your cheerleading coach or trainer to see if this is something you should consider adding to your shoes.

Keep first aid kits with ice, plastic bags, and elastic bandages on hand so that common injuries like muscle strains, twists, or pulls can be treated immediately. Your coach should already have these nearby in case of an emergency, but you can check to see if this has been done or whether you should supply your own.

Injuries may prevent you from fully participating in cheerleading events on occasion. In times when you are limited by injury, you will probably have to wear a bandage, brace, or some other form of support to keep a muscle or joint as still as possible to avoid making it worse or reinjuring it. For example, a cheerleader who has problems with a knee, or who is recovering from a knee injury, may wear a special knee brace and avoid doing certain tumbling moves or jumps so that he or she does not

Compression bandages are worn to support injured joints in the event of twists or sprains.

damage the knee any further. Someone else may wear an ankle brace to support a twisted ankle that is still healing.

Be sure to wear braces or supports exactly as your doctor orders. Do not avoid wearing them just because they make your uniform look "bulky" or don't "go with it." The most important thing is the safety and health of your body, and it is better to put up with a bulky uniform than risk serious injury. After all, you may not only make your injury worse, but you could also cause enough damage that you are not able to participate at all—perhaps even permanently.

TEXT-DEPENDENT QUESTIONS:

1. Name three examples of leg and ankle stretches that cheerleaders should do before practice or competition.

2. What is an exercise you can do to build strength in your hamstrings?

3. What is the most important part of the cheerleader's uniform, and why?

RESEARCH PROJECT:

Look into what is required to put together an effective off-season training program. What types of activities are best to keep squad members in shape? How might off-season training vary from your in-season program?

WORDS TO UNDERSTAND:

aesthetic: concerned with beauty or the appreciation of beauty

limber: (of a person or body part) lithe; having a supple and resilient quality

vertebrae: small bones that are linked together to form the backbone

Chapter 4

TAKING CARE OF THE BODY: INJURIES AND NUTRITION

Like athletes in any other highly physical sport, cheerleaders are prone to injury. That's why it's so important to take the time to warm up; however, even with proper preparation, injuries can—and do—happen. This chapter will present an overview of some of the most common injuries suffered by cheerleaders. But remember—no book can take the place of a consultation with your coach or doctor.

In cheerleading competitions, and especially during sporting events like football games, there are often long periods of time in which cheerleaders are simply standing around waiting. Keep your muscles warm, and stay **limber** during these times so you do not injure yourself when cheerleading begins again.

> *Cheerleading has long periods of waiting around to either compete or to cheer. Cheerleaders should be mindful of letting their muscles get too cool and tight.*

Studies show some of the most common injuries cheerleaders suffer are pulled muscles, inflamed tendons, and sprained ligaments. Hip and groin injuries also happen frequently. Furthermore, certain cheerleading routines, such as pyramids or partner stunts, are more dangerous (e.g., one cheerleader standing on the shoulders of another cheerleader and then performing a gymnastic maneuver off her shoulders). Accidents during these stunts can cause serious head injuries or broken necks. Cheerleaders have even died from falling from the upper part of a pyramid. As a result, some schools have banned these high-risk activities.

HEAD AND NECK INJURIES

CONCUSSION

Blows to the head, even ones that do not look that forceful, can result in a concussion, which is technically a traumatic injury to the brain. It may upset your thinking, sight, and balance, and you may even become unconscious.

How much force was applied to the head and at what angle the head was struck are determining factors in the degree of concussion. If the injured

person regains consciousness fairly quickly, that is a good sign. Even so, the person should be watched for symptoms such as headache, nausea, or further loss of consciousness, which can indicate bleeding inside the head. If the loss of consciousness lasts for a significant amount of time, or if the person does not recover consciousness at all, the injured person must be taken to a hospital for immediate treatment. Doctors will insist that under no

With all of its high-risk maneuvers, falls are part of cheerleading, and unfortunately, so are concussions.

circumstances should a person who has suffered even a minor concussion be allowed to participate in any physical activity for at least twenty-four hours after the injury.

Concussions result in different degrees of brain swelling, meaning the skull exerts pressure on the brain. This swelling must be given a chance to go down completely because another blow—even a small one—could cause serious damage to the brain.

WHIPLASH

Whiplash is the painful strain of neck muscles and ligaments caused by sudden, violent movement. This can happen if a person is pushed suddenly from behind. Whiplash can be a severe injury, and if you have this kind of injury, you should consult a doctor who can then perform X-rays to make sure that the delicate **vertebrae** in your neck have not slipped out of alignment or become fractured.

Rest, anti-inflammatory medication, and sometimes physical therapy, where needed, is the course of treatment for whiplash. Some patients also need to wear a cervical collar, which is a high collar that supports the weight of the head, thereby taking the strain off the ligaments.

BACK INJURIES

Muscle sprains and strains in the back are also common in cheerleading. Just because these injuries are common, however, doesn't make them any less serious. One of the most dangerous back injuries is a "slipped" disk in the spine. This happens when the disk that acts as a cushion between two vertebrae bulges out from in between them, putting pressure on a nerve.

Never take the assessment of an injury from a coach or other nonmedical person as a diagnosis, no matter how much experience he or she may have. It is always best to see a doctor when any injuries happen. This is especially true in the case of back injuries because X-rays and other diagnostic tests may be needed to determine exactly what has happened and what needs to be treated.

The typical course of treatment for strains and sprains is to keep the patient

Tumbling is one of the activities in cheerleading that can result in back strains.

as still as possible and alternate treating the affected area with a heating pad and ice packs for fifteen to thirty minutes at a time. An anti-inflammatory medication, such as ibuprofen, may be administered. Treatment from a licensed massage therapist may also be helpful.

SHOULDER INJURIES

Due to its unique design, the shoulder is more unstable than many other joints. The shoulder is the only joint in the human body that is not held together by its ligaments. The few ligaments that are there serve only to keep it from moving too far in any one direction.

Rotator cuff tears are a common shoulder injury experienced by cheerleaders. Sports in which the arms are constantly brought up over the head, as in cheerleading, can put too much stress on the shoulder joint, and the rotator cuff muscles can stretch out, causing the ball of the joint to become loose inside the shoulder socket. As a result, tendons rub against the bone and become inflamed and painful. Most people with a rotator cuff injury report feeling pain in their biceps or deep within their shoulder joint.

Unfortunately, rotator cuff injuries are commonly misdiagnosed as strains

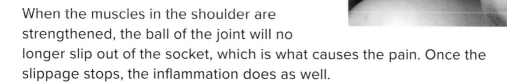

Shoulder problems like rotator cuff injuries are not uncommon in cheerleading and other activities that require repeatedly bringing the arm over the head.

or tendonitis (inflamed tendons). Doctors will provide medication, such as cortisone injections, to treat inflammation, and the athlete is advised to rest the shoulder. Reducing inflammation will decrease pain, but it will not, however, treat the actual problem— the slippage of the joint—so once the person begins cheering again, the pain will return unless it is given enough time to heal.

When the muscles in the shoulder are strengthened, the ball of the joint will no longer slip out of the socket, which is what causes the pain. Once the slippage stops, the inflammation does as well.

Surgery may be necessary if other initial courses of treatment do not work. The surgery will repair the torn tendon. Afterward, the person will need physical therapy and rest from cheerleading to ensure complete recovery. When surgery is not prescribed, physical therapy can often help heal the injury enough to continue with physical activity.

WRIST INJURIES

Wrists are among the weakest of all the joints. Cheerleaders in particular are susceptible to wrist injuries because there is so much pressure put on them due to the gymnastic aspect of cheerleading. Cartwheels, roundoffs, back handsprings—all these maneuvers put an extraordinary amount of weight on the wrists, causing them to be more vulnerable to accidents.

As with any other sprain, treating a sprained wrist typically includes keeping the joint still and rested. Also, be sure to apply ice packs at regular intervals for fifteen to thirty minutes at a time for three to four days. Sometimes, a soft splint is also required to help keep the joint in place while it recovers. To avoid a wrist injury altogether, pay close attention to the wrists during warm-up.

Cheerleading stunts are impressive to watch. Pint-sized, dynamo flyers are tossed ten to twenty feet (three to nine meters) into the air and caught in carefully choreographed precision movements. That is when everything is executed well. To train to get to that point, however, these girls with no safety equipment suffer dozens of falls and drops in practice. Among the high school sports reporting catastrophic injuries like brain damage and paralysis, cheerleading is second only to football and accounts for two-thirds of catastrophic injuries to girls. The American Academy of Pediatrics, reacting to the more than 38,000 annual emergency room visits related to cheerleading, released these recommendations to improve safety for these athletes:

- Cheerleading should be designated as a sport in all states, allowing for benefits such as qualified coaches, better access to medical care, and injury surveillance.

- All cheerleaders should have a pre-season physical as well as access to qualified strength and conditioning coaches.

- Cheerleaders should be trained in all spotting techniques and attempt stunts only after demonstrating appropriate skill progression.

- Pyramid and partner stunts should be performed only on a spring or foam floor, grass, or turf. Stunts should never be performed on hard, wet, or uneven surfaces. Pyramids should not be more than two people high.

- Coaches, parents, and athletes should have access to a written emergency plan.

- Any cheerleader suspected of having a head injury should be removed from practice or competition and not allowed to return until he or she has clearance from a health professional.

GROIN INJURIES

The adductor muscles along the inside of the upper thighs are the muscles in the groin that pull the legs together when they contract and also help stabilize the hip joints.

Cheerleading maneuvers make its athletes especially susceptible to groin pulls. A pull in a muscle occurs when it has been stretched too far (which can happen when someone attempts a split or a high kick without first properly warming up). Typical symptoms of a groin pull include pain, swelling, bruising, and tenderness, specifically when stretching.

Once again, resting the injury for several days (doctors may recommend at least one week of rest) is the recommended course of treatment. Icing the groin to reduce swelling and wrapping it with a compression bandage are also recommended.

KNEE INJURIES

The knee is an intricate network of muscles, tendons, ligaments, cartilage, and bone, which assists us in a variety of motions. This complex joint is the most commonly injured in the body, accounting for about one-fourth of all sports-related injuries.

One of the worst knee injuries cheerleaders suffer is a tear in the anterior cruciate ligament (A.C.L.) on the front of the knee, which provides support and stability in the knee joint. An A.C.L. tear is a serious injury and not something that can be treated at home. It most often occurs when the

With all the jumping and landing involved, the knees take a beating in cheerleading.

knee is hit by a strong force, in the middle of a twisting motion during a fall, or when someone falls heavily against someone or something.

In the case of an A.C.L. strain, physical therapy alone may repair the damage. However, if the A.C.L. ruptures and tears completely, which is what often happens, surgery is usually needed, followed by extensive physical therapy. A brace may also be worn for some time to give the knee additional support. You may be able to return to your cheerleading activities but only after a sufficient rest period under the guidance of your doctor or coach.

HAMSTRING INJURIES

The hamstrings are the muscles at the back of the thigh. Hamstring pulls are among the most common muscle pulls and are usually caused by failing to warm up properly. Typical symptoms of a hamstring pull can include sharp pain and swelling and, in the most severe tears, bruising due to internal bleeding within the muscle. You may also be unable to raise your leg straight off the ground more than a short distance without feeling pain. Typical treatment includes rest, ice, and compression, which means resting for at least two or three days; icing the muscle for twenty minutes, three to four times a day; and wrapping the muscle in a compression bandage.

ANKLE INJURIES

Cheerleading is tough on the ankles, and sprains are common. Ankles are sprained when the ligaments are stretched too far and tear. When treating an ankle sprain, a doctor may recommend that you keep the foot rested for a least the first twenty-four hours, placing no weight on the ankle if

Cheerleaders need to have strong ankles to reduce the chance of injury. Ankle injuries are among the most common in cheerleading.

at all possible (which may mean you have to use crutches). An ankle sprain is often accompanied by a great deal of swelling, so you may be told to ice the ankle for twenty minutes, remove the ice for twenty minutes, ice it again, and so on, for at least the first forty-eight hours or until the ankle returns to normal size. You may also be advised to wrap the ankle with a compression bandage and keep it elevated higher than your heart by propping it up on pillows at night to reduce swelling and bruising. Typically, after a couple of days, you may be able to put weight on the ankle again.

> Breakfast is my favorite meal of the day. I try to keep it healthy by eating fresh fruit because it's sweet and nutritious. You can also add a carbohydrate in there like a bagel or croissant for energy.
>
> – Maddie Gardner, two-time USASF All Star world champion

NUTRITION

The way you choose to fuel your body is just as important as how you maintain and prepare it. All athletes, including cheerleaders, must be careful to eat a proper blend of nutrients to make sure their bodies and minds perform as well as they possibly can. This doesn't just mean eating healthy foods but also choosing when to eat, how much to eat, and whether to take dietary supplements. Of course, when you choose a new diet or supplements, you should consult with a nutritionist, doctor, or some other expert. Don't make up your own nutritional program!

WHAT TO EAT

Although a balanced diet is important for everyone, it is even more important for athletes. Typically, an athlete has to eat considerably more than a normal person. The United States Food and Drug Administration (FDA) suggests that the average American should eat about 2,000 calories a day; for a male high school- or college-level athlete, a diet averaging 3,000 to 4,000 calories is more common. For female athletes, the range is about 2,500 to 3,000 calories. The higher the physical intensity of the sport, the higher the calorie requirement. There are three main food groups to consider when choosing a diet: carbohydrates, protein, and fats.

A physical therapist gives tips for injury prevention for cheerleading

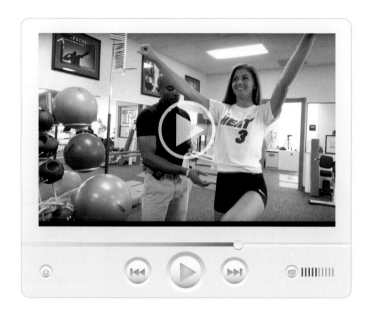

CARBOHYDRATES

Starchy foods contain carbohydrates, which is what the body breaks down to get energy. Starchy foods include breads and grains, vegetables such as potatoes, cereal, pasta, and rice. There is no one-size-fits-all formula that can exactly dictate what an athlete's carb consumption should be. A general rule is that in season or during times of intense training, athletes should eat about 5 grams (0.2 ounces) of carbs for every pound (0.5 kilogram) of body weight. In the off-season or during periods of lower training levels, it should be about 2 to 3 grams (0.07–0.10 ounces) per pound. The body uses carbs strictly for fuel, so if they are not being burned, they are turned into fat and stored. Therefore it is important to adjust carb intake based on activity level. Athletes should not eat heavily processed carbohydrates such as white sugar and white flour. These simple carbs are quickly broken down into sugars, which the body processes into fats if it does not immediately burn them off. The best carbohydrate choices for an athlete are complex types like pasta and whole-grain foods as well as starchy vegetables. A nutritious diet avoids empty calories or those provided by food that lacks other nourishment, like processed sugar and starches.

Cheerleaders should try to eat about half a gram of protein per day for every pound of body weight to maintain good muscle mass.

PROTEIN

Unlike carbohydrates, protein is used within the body. Proteins are important chemicals used to perform specific functions inside the body's cells. Our bodies can break down proteins that are found in foods and use them to build new proteins that make up our muscles and bones. During periods of intense training and activity, the body needs more protein to repair damage to muscles. Not eating enough protein can cause an athlete to lose muscle mass and negatively affect the ability to perform. The Academy of Nutrition and Dietetics recommends athletes consume about 0.50 to 0.75 grams (0.02–0.03 ounce) of protein for every pound (0.5 kilogram) of body weight. During the season or heavy training, that number should be closer to a full gram (0.04 ounce) per pound. This higher ratio is also true if an athlete is trying to build muscle mass. The best sources of proteins are lean meats and dairy products (such as milk or cheese) as well as eggs and certain types of soy, beans, and nuts.

FATS

Lots of times, we think of fats as bad for us because eating too much of them is unhealthy. However, fat is an important ingredient needed to make our bodies work correctly. They help balance hormone production, support cell growth, and protect our organs, among other functions. Without fats, our bodies cannot absorb certain vitamins as well as they should. Also, our skin and hair need some amount of fat to grow correctly. However, fat should still be eaten in moderation as it is higher in calories than protein or carbs. No more than 70 grams (2.5 ounces) a day is recommended. All fats are not created equal, however. Trans fats and saturated fats found in processed foods are high in bad cholesterol, which clogs arteries and is bad for the heart. The best sources of fat are vegetable oils, olive oil, and nuts.

DIETARY SUPPLEMENTS

Ideally, a balanced diet would provide our bodies with all the nutrients it needs. However, due to many varying factors, eating optimally is not always possible. Dietary supplements are available to fill dietary gaps created by a deficient diet.

In discussing dietary supplements here, this does not include banned performance-enhancing substances. Instead, the focus is on supplements that contain vitamins, minerals, and other compounds that help the

Vitamin tablets should never take the place of eating healthy meals but can be used to supplement diets that are lacking certain nutrients.

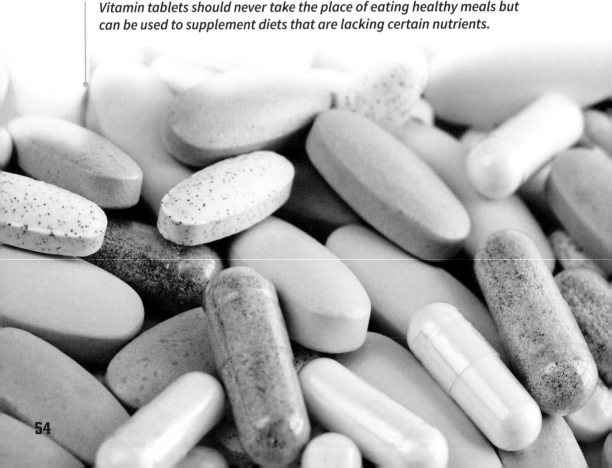

body absorb nutrients or recover more efficiently. When properly used supplements can improve overall health and performance, but you should always consult a doctor or other expert before using them to augment your diet or training program. Some examples of common supplements include vitamin tablets and protein shakes or powder.

VITAMIN TABLETS

For many reasons, we do not always get the vitamins and nutrients we need. Often, this is because our diets are not as balanced as they should be. Sometimes, it is because the foods that are available to us have been processed in such a way that they lose nutrients. If you know or suspect that a certain key vitamin is underrepresented in what you are eating, in many cases, the necessary vitamins can be obtained from vitamin supplements. These supplements, which are usually taken as a pill, can either contain a balanced mixture of vitamins and nutrients (multivitamins) or contain a single vitamin or mineral that the diet is lacking. The best way to avoid this issue is to work hard to eat right whenever possible.

PROTEIN SUPPLEMENTS

Getting enough protein from the food you eat can be difficult as well. For athletes, eating protein immediately after a workout is recommended (to refuel the body), but most people either don't feel up to or do not have the time to spend cooking or preparing themselves a meal immediately after a workout or competition. That is where protein shakes come in handy. These are protein supplements sold in powder form that look and taste like milkshakes when blended with water but contain no dairy products. Protein shakes deliver a high ratio of protein to carbohydrates and calories. They are not meant to replace meals. Many other necessary nutrients are gained from a balanced diet that cannot be replaced by protein shakes, regardless of how fortified they may be.

STAYING HYDRATED

The body needs water more than it needs any other nutrient. If you are not getting enough water, your performance will suffer in spite of any preparation or balanced diet. Dehydration occurs when your body doesn't have enough water. Symptoms include fatigue, dizziness, and headaches. No athlete can perform at his or her best if not properly hydrated. Proper hydration should be maintained not only at competitions but throughout training as well. The body does not store water, so we need to constantly maintain its supply. The American College of Sports Medicine recommends these guidelines for athletes:

- Before Exercise: Drink 16 to 20 ounces (473–591 milliliters) within the two-hour period prior to exercise.

- During Exercise: Drink 4 to 8 ounces (118–237 milliliters) every fifteen to twenty minutes during exercise.

- Post Exercise: Replace 24 ounces (710 milliliters) for every pound (0.5 kilogram) of body weight lost during exercise

Cheerleading is an **aesthetic** sport, meaning that importance is placed on the appearance of the body, and it is judged in competition with an aesthetic component. Parents and coaches must be careful about the message they send about appearance. It is not uncommon for athletes to resort to drastic measures to meet the perceived aesthetic characteristics of cheerleading. This can lead to serious growth and development concerns as well as nutritional deficiencies and disordered eating. Athletic performance should be emphasized over weight and body composition, and to perform well, the body needs fuel. Stick to a nutrition plan that promotes healthy eating behaviors.

Water is the body's most crucial nutrient, and cheerleaders should drink plenty of it.

TEXT-DEPENDENT QUESTIONS:

1. What do studies show are some of the most common injuries cheerleaders suffer?

2. Name some typical symptoms of a groin pull.

3. List three examples of carbohydrates.

RESEARCH PROJECT:

Put together a sample nutrition plan for yourself by mapping out meals and snacks for a given week. Pick a week when you are training and competing. Be sure to consider the nutrition benefits of everything you choose as well as the time it will take to make the plan work in your busy schedule. Don't forget to include a hydration schedule.

WORDS TO UNDERSTAND:

orchestrated: organized or planned (something that is complicated)

predominantly: for the most part

spectrum: a complete range of different opinions, people, etc.

Chapter 5

CHEERLEADING: POM-POMS, PYRAMIDS, AND PERCEPTION

SIS BOOM BAH TO VARSITY SPIRIT

"Rah, rah, rah! Ski-u-mah! Hoo-rah! Hoo-rah! Varsity! Varsity! Minnesota!"

This is believed to be the first-ever organized cheer, led by University of Minnesota medical student John Campbell at a football game in November 1898. Cheerleading is closely associated with the rise of football in America. The idea of cheering traces back to Thomas Peebles, who came to the University of Minnesota after graduating from Princeton University in 1882. At Princeton, Peebles had been part of an all-male pep club. At Princeton, cheers from the crowd could be heard at both football and baseball games. There was the Tiger and Rocket cheer as well as the Princeton cheer, parts of both which still exist in the current day Locomotive cheer:

"Rah, rah, rah! Tiger, tiger tiger! Sis, sis, sis! Boom, boom boom, ah! Princeton! Princeton! Princeton!"

The first organized cheer is believed to have happened at a football game at the University of Minnesota in 1898.

Peebles brought the tradition of crowd cheers to Minnesota in 1894, and after Campbell **orchestrated** having his group lead the crowd in cheering four years later, the activity of cheerleading was born.

This probably does not sound much like what most people think of when they consider cheerleading and the cheerleaders of today. There were, in fact, no female cheerleaders until 1923, when women were permitted to join the team at Minnesota.

One of the early innovations in the art of getting a whole stadium of people to follow along with cheers was the introduction of flash cards. This is often credited as coming from Oregon State University (OSU) in 1923, but in fact, it came to OSU that year when Lindley Bothwell brought the idea from the University of Southern California (USC). Bothwell was "yell king" at USC. He would have 2,500-person sections trained to form letters and designs on demand with large flash cards. By 1945 many of the West Coast schools were well-known for their flash card stunts.

That year also saw a significant shift in the makeup of cheerleading teams. Due to the fact that most college-age men left campuses to fight in World

In the 1940s, cheerleading permanently shifted from a mostly male to a mostly female activity.

Lawrence Herkimer, the grandfather of cheerleading, was the head cheerleader at Southern Methodist University in the late 1940s.

War II, teams went from **predominantly** male to mostly female by 1945 (Today, more than 90 percent of all cheerleaders are women.) Despite this, it was a man who came up with perhaps the best-known move in cheerleading.

Lawrence Herkimer was the head cheerleader at Southern Methodist University (SMU). He graduated in 1948 and took a job as a physical education and statistics teacher at his alma mater. That same summer, he decided to put on a cheerleading camp to teach kids what he knew. He had 52 girls and one boy sign up. The next summer, Herkimer founded the National Cheerleaders Association (NCA) and got 350 students to attend his clinic at Sam Houston State. He eventually quit his job at SMU to teach cheerleading full time.

> I was making more money in the summertime in camps than I was teaching all year at SMU. So I quit teaching and went full time into cheerleading. It grew by leaps and bounds.
>
> – Lawrence Herkimer, the grandfather of cheerleading

Herkimer, who is often referred to as the grandfather of cheerleading, went on to turn it into a multi-million-dollar enterprise. Under the umbrella of the NCA, clinics would eventually be held at 430 locations across the country every year, with 150,000 attendees annually.

Herkimer started the Cheerleader Supply Company, which published a catalog offering everything from uniforms and badges to sample cheers and instructions. He would eventually publish an instruction manual called *The Complete Book of Cheerleading* in 1975. He developed the spirit stick and, in anticipation of the popularity of sports on color TV, the pom-pom, which he patented in 1971.

Herkimer may eventually best be remembered for his signature move, developed during his cheerleader days at SMU and taught at NCA camps. The Herkie is a jump that has been used at the culmination of cheer routines for decades. The one fist on the hip, the other raised in the air, half-split jump is the logo to his legacy. Herkimer sold his cheerleading empire for $20 million in 1986 (about $44 million in 2017 dollars). He died in 2015 at age 89.

The man who would eventually come to own Herkimer's former companies is a former instructor at one of his NCA camps. Jeff Webb was also a former employee of Herkimer's after graduating from the University of Oklahoma, where he was a yell leader. After three years with Herkimer, Webb left to found his own company, the Universal Cheerleaders Association, in 1974. The company soon became known as Varsity Spirit.

Varsity Spirit was largely responsible for raising the profile of cheerleading to a national level and driving the development of it as a competitive, dance-based, athletic activity. In less than ten years, Webb had Varsity-sponsored national cheerleading competitions televised on the cable sports network ESPN. Today, Varsity continues to drive the competitive side of the industry while also supporting more traditional cheerleading.

SCHOOL SQUADS AND ALL STARS

Traditionally, the scholastic variety is what most people think of when they hear the word "cheerleading." Scholastic cheerleaders are associated with a school at the middle school, high school, or college level. They primarily cheer at the events or games played by the teams and athletes from the school. Scholastic cheerleaders may also attend rallies or other events aimed at raising school spirit.

Scholastic cheerleaders do have to participate in tryouts and be selected to make their cheerleading squads. At the high school level, there are often two levels, varsity and junior varsity. Criteria for consideration varies from school to school, as does the sophistication of the program. At some schools, the level of difficulty of cheers and routines is quite basic, consisting simply of ground-based dances and limited routines.

At the other end of the **spectrum**, some programs have an advanced level of difficulty with acrobatics, including flips, lifts, and precision choreography. Schools at this level are the ones most likely to compete to qualify for the UCA National High School Cheerleading Championships, a Varsity-run event. The event includes several categories, including coed, and is categorized by division and school size. The event was first held in 1980. Today, event finals are held at Walt Disney World in Orlando, Florida, and televised internationally. In 2016, 680 teams from thirty-one states competed across all categories.

The UCA also has a college competition with six divisions: Division 1A coed, Division 1 coed, Division II and Open Coed, Division 1A All Girl, Division I All Girl, and Open All Girl. More than fifty schools

Scholastic cheerleaders perform during halftime at a high school basketball game.

were represented across the six divisions in 2017. The University of Kentucky competes in the Division IA Coed category, where the program has dominated for decades.

Kentucky has won twenty-two UCA National College Cheerleading championships, including eight straight from 1995 to 2002. The Wildcats have also finished second six times. Head coach Jomo Thompson, who won four championships as a squad member and, as of 2017, twelve more as a coach, leads the Wildcats program.

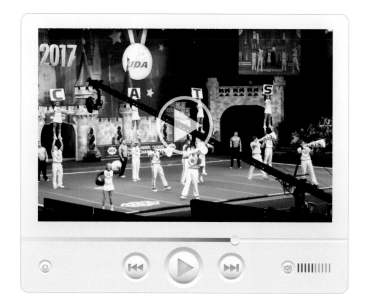

Watch the University of Kentucky cheerleaders perform their 2017 national championship routine.

The other prominent division of cheerleading is All Star cheerleading. Unlike scholastic cheerleading, All Star cheerleading squads are not affiliated with schools, and therefore you will not find them cheering on the sidelines at football or basketball games. All Star squads are privately funded and operate out of private gyms or clubs that often also teach dance and gymnastics. These are competitive teams that enter events sponsored by the United States All Star Federation (USASF).

The USASF was founded in 2003 to represent a number of different organizations as the national governing body for All Star cheerleading. All Star cheerleading had received recognition as a separate entity from

scholastic cheerleading in 1987, when the NCA created a separate All Star competition. All Star clubs grew in popularity into the 1990s, but there was no uniform set of judging rules to adhere to, and clubs or regional competitions had their own sets of regulations, making it difficult to have a true standard. The USASF served to create a standard set of rules that must be followed by any competition that wants to be sanctioned by the federation.

Since 2004, the USASF has hosted the World Cheerleading Championships, also held in Orlando. This competition is strictly for senior level five and six All Star squads who must qualify to get into the event. The Cheerleading Worlds, as the event is commonly called, attracts more than 9,000 cheer athletes representing clubs from forty countries to compete.

SIDEBAR
Jamie Andries

Cheerleaders might not have the high profile that other athletes like quarterbacks or pitchers might. But cheer does have its share of superstars. The brightest of these may be Texan Jamie Andries. Andries is a bona-fide cheerleading celebrity, or "cheerlebrity," as the Internet calls her. She started posting on her Instagram account in high school, including some personal photos but mostly cheerleading-related ones. Cheerleading fans flocked to her page in droves, along with a handful of other teenage cheerleading phenoms. By the time she was sixteen, Andries had more than 400,000 followers. By the time she graduated a year early to go to the University of Oklahoma (yes, she is on the cheerleading squad at OU), she had well over half a million followers. *New York Magazine* deemed Andries "the alpha girl of Instagram" in a 2014 profile.

These cheerlebrities have earned the devotion of their fans with extraordinary skill. Andries, who performed in All Star competitions with her teammates from Cheer Athletics in Plano, Texas, won both NCA and world championships. Her talent as a flyer is clear, and the dedication to cheerleading that would be required to be so good is substantial. Andries takes being a cheerlebrity in stride, simply saying, "It's fun while it lasts."

The international governing body for All Star cheerleading is the International Cheer Union (ICU), which is another Varsity entity founded in 2004 and headed by Webb himself. The organization, run as a nonprofit and 110-member federation, advocates for groups that "positively advance cheerleading throughout the world." A twelve-person governing council that represents various geographic areas runs the ICU.

The ICU holds its own set of World Championships in Orlando each year. Unlike the USASF Cheerleading Worlds, the athletes do not represent

In 2010, a U.S. District court ruled that competitive cheer is not a sport in part because it is not recognized as such by the NCAA.

their local clubs. Rather, at the ICU event they represent their countries as national teams. The USASF event determines the best All Star club in the world, while the ICU event determines the best All Star country. The 2017 ICU World Cheerleading Championships had representation from forty countries. Competitions were held in the coed and all-girl categories.

THE NCAA AND THE OLYMPICS

Is cheerleading a sport? The organizations that run it are certainly trying to remove any doubts that it is. These efforts, however, do not involve the cheerleading found on football sidelines and basketball halftime shows. Cheerleading officials are promoting what Webb calls "modern athletic cheerleading," such as the type found in the All Star category.

The National Collegiate Athletic Association (NCAA) runs college athletics in the United States. To the NCAA, cheerleading has been the crowd-energizing activities performed on the sidelines of games; simply put cheerleading supported athletic events. It was not one itself but rather an extracurricular activity. In fact, in 2010, a U.S. District Court in Connecticut ruled that competitive cheer was not a sport in part because it is not recognized as such by the NCAA.

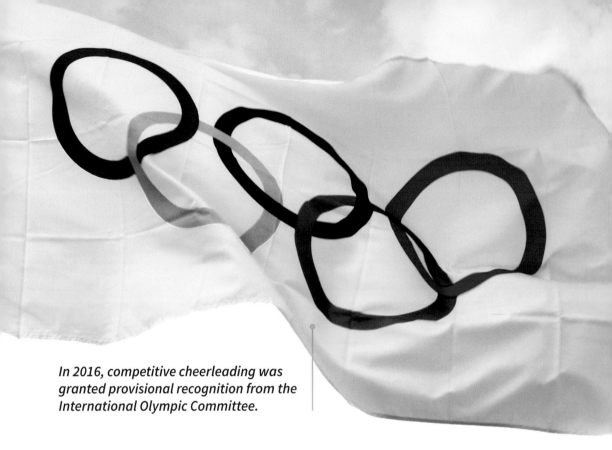

In 2016, competitive cheerleading was granted provisional recognition from the International Olympic Committee.

Enter STUNT. STUNT positions itself as a the modern evolution of cheerleading. According to the STUNT website, STUNT "removes the crowd-leading element and focuses on the technical and athletic components of cheer, including partner stunts, pyramids, basket tosses, group jumps and tumbling." STUNT is set up as a competition with four quarters where teams take turns doing routines and are scored on the number and kinds of mistakes they make. The team with the best score after four quarters wins. STUNT was created as part of the NCAA's initiative called Emerging Sport. This initiative recognizes developing women's sports and looks to help schools provide more opportunities for female athletes in these sports. There were nine emerging sports identified when the initiative was announced. Five have since achieved NCAA championship status: beach volleyball, rowing, ice hockey, water polo, and bowling. Over the years, sports were added to or removed from the list, with each addition getting ten years to get to championship status.

STUNT was added to the list in 2011 as USA Cheer, the cheerleading's overall national governing body, actively lobbied for its new creation to be recognized as a sport. STUNT participation is now at more than fifty universities, and it continues to meet the minimum standard for NCAA status each year as it awaits recognition for championship status. Unlike traditional cheerleading, which USA Cheer wants to preserve, STUNT's exclusive purpose is competition. It has a fully developed regular and postseason schedule (unlike All Star cheer, which builds toward one main annual competition), an objective and consistent scoring system, and is regulated by a national governing body.

The ICU took a big step forward in December of 2016 toward having competitive cheer recognized as a sport when it achieved provisional recognition from the International Olympic Committee (IOC). This means that cheerleading has three years to promote itself with IOC-assisted funding, during which the ICU can apply for full recognition. To be clear, the competitive cheerleading version the ICU is promoting for inclusion is not STUNT, the NCAA version of competitive cheer. This is due to a dispute with Fédération Internationale de Gymnastique (FIG), the international gymnastics federation. FIG opposed cheerleading's application, arguing that cheerleading needed to maintain some of its cheer characteristics, such as a spirit yell, to remain distinct from gymnastics, which of course also included a lot of tumbling and acrobatics.

This appears to be a 180-degree shift for Webb, the head of the ICU. Webb testified in that 2010 Connecticut court case mentioned earlier as an expert witness, declaring that cheerleading was not a sport. As recently as 2015, Webb sent lobbyists from Varsity to fight a bill in California that would have designated cheerleading as a sport. The bill, AB 949, did pass, and cheerleading is now a sport in California. Official guidelines for safety and coaching were due to be established in 2017.

At issue for Webb and Varsity is that official designation comes with more regulations, which could include participation limits. This would affect the time athletes would be allowed to spend on cheerleading activities in the off-season, including Varsity's highly profitable cheerleading camps. Recognition by the IOC, however, would not carry the same impact as it would coming from the NCAA or the National Federation of State High School Associations.

One organization that has declared cheerleading to be a sport is the American Medical Association. The group announced in 2014 that cheerleading should be added to the roster of sports due to its rigorous physical nature. The group of physicians has specific motives behind the designation, however. If cheerleading is declared to be an official sport, that would come with regulated safety measures and mandatory safety training for coaches.

Will either the NCAA or the IOC recognize competitive cheerleading as a sport in the near future? That remains to be seen. The National Association of Intercollegiate Athletics (NAIA) is an association of smaller four-year schools about one-fifth the size of the NCAA and mostly located in the western part of the country. In August of 2016, the NAIA voted to make competitive cheer a championship sport. The rest of the organized sports world may not be far behind.

Thousands of young girls attend Varsity Spirit cheerleading camps every year, a scenario that might be in jeopardy if cheerleading is declared a sport in the United States.

TEXT-DEPENDENT QUESTIONS:

1. Explain how cheerleading was born.

2. What is the difference between scholastic cheerleading and All Star cheerleading?

3. In what year was STUNT added to the NCAA's emerging sports initiative?

RESEARCH PROJECT:

Look up the rules and regulations for STUNT. STUNT was created to try and give cheerleading competitions more of a traditional sports structure. Come up with your own ideas of ways to incorporate elements of traditional sports into cheerleading, and create the outline for your own new sport.

SERIES GLOSSARY OF KEY TERMS

Acute Injury: usually the result of a specific impact or traumatic event that occurs in one specific area of the body, such as a muscle, bone, or joint.

Calories: units of heat used to indicate the amount of energy that foods will produce in the human body.

Carbohydrates: substances found in certain foods (such as bread, rice, and potatoes) that provide the body with heat and energy and are made of carbon, hydrogen, and oxygen.

Cardiovascular: of or relating to the heart and blood vessels.

Concussion: a stunning, damaging, or shattering effect from a hard blow—especially a jarring injury of the brain resulting in a disturbance of cerebral function.

Confidence: faith in oneself and one's abilities without any suggestion of conceit or arrogance.

Cooldown: easy exercise, done after more intense activity, to allow the body to gradually transition to a resting or near-resting state.

Dietary Supplements: products taken orally that contain one or more ingredient (such as vitamins or amino acids) that are intended to supplement one's diet and are not considered food.

Dynamic: having active strength of body or mind.

Electrolytes: substances (such as sodium or calcium) that are ions in the body regulating the flow of nutrients into and waste products out of cells.

Flexible: applies to something that can be readily bent, twisted, or folded without any sign of injury.

Hamstrings: any of three muscles at the back of the thigh that function to flex and rotate the leg and extend the thigh.

Hydration: to supply with ample fluid or moisture.

Imagery: mental images, the products of imagination.

Mind-Set: a mental attitude or inclination.

Overuse Injury: an injury that is most likely to occur to the ankles, knees, hands, and wrists, due to the excessive use of these body parts during exercise and athletics.

Plyometrics: also known as "jump training" or "plyos," exercises in which muscles exert maximum force in short intervals of time, with the goal of increasing power (speed and strength).

Positive Mental Attitude (PMA): the philosophy that having an optimistic disposition in every situation in one's life attracts positive changes and increases achievement.

Protein: a nutrient found in food (as in meat, milk, eggs, and beans) that is made up of many amino acids joined together, is a necessary part of the diet, and is essential for normal cell structure and function.

Quadriceps: the greater extensor muscle of the front of the thigh that is divided into four parts.

Recovery: the act or process of becoming healthy after an illness or injury.

Resistance: relating to exercise, involving pushing against a source of resistance (such as a weight) to increase strength. Strength training, or resistance exercises, are those that build muscle. They create stronger and larger muscles by producing more and tougher muscle fibers to cope with the increasing weight demands.

Strategy: a careful plan or method.

Stretching: to extend one's body or limbs from a cramped, stooping, or relaxed position.

Tactics: actions or methods that are planned and used to achieve a particular goal.

Tendon: a tough piece of tissue in the body that connects a muscle to a bone.

Training: the process by which an athlete prepares for competition by exercising, practicing, and so on.

Warm-Up: exercise or practice especially before a game or contest—broadly, to get ready.

Workout: a practice or exercise to test or improve one's fitness for athletic competition, ability, or performance.

FURTHER READING:

Maurer, Tracy & Davis, Lauren. *Cheerleading Gear (Jump and Shout)*. Audible Studios on Brilliance Audio, 2017.

Headridge, Pam & Webb, Robb. *101 Cheerleading Drills*. Monterey, CA. Coaches Choice, 2014.

The Editors of Varsity. *Varsity's Ultimate Guide to Cheerleading*. Poppy, 2014.

Skinner, Alton. *Winning Cardio Strength Workouts for Cheerleaders*. Eight Count Media, 2013

INTERNET RESOURCES:

College STUNT Association: *http://collegestunt.org/*

Universal Cheerleaders Association: *https://uca.varsity.com/*

Stop Sports Injuries: *http://www.stopsportsinjuries.org/STOP/Prevent_ Injuries/Cheerleading_Injury_Prevention.aspx?WebsiteKey=22144c04- 3260-4510-b318-8b5768345a42*

FDA, Dietary Supplements: *http://www.fda.gov/Food/DietarySupplements/default.htm*

VIDEO CREDITS:

Watch a routine from 2017 NCA All Star national champions Top Gun from Miami. *https://www.youtube.com/watch?v=Uf3Pa0lz92g*

Registered dietician and former college competitive cheerleader Nicole Aucoin offers tips on what to eat before a workout. *http://x-qr.net/1HYB*

Check out these stretching tips for cheerleaders from world champion All Star cheerleader Gabi Butler. *http://x-qr.net/1EmG*

A physical therapist gives tips for injury prevention for cheerleading. *http://x-qr.net/1Gcz*

Watch the University of Kentucky cheerleaders perform their 2017 national championship routine. *http://x-qr.net/1Ddx*

PICTURE CREDITS

QR CODES AND LINKS TO THIRD-PARTY CONTENT

INDEX

In this index, page numbers in **bold italics** font indicate photos or videos.

ABOUT THE AUTHOR

Peter Douglas is a former journalist, reporting on both sports and general news for many years at television stations in various locations across the US affiliated with NBC, CBS and Fox. Prior to his journalism career he worked with the Boston Red Sox Major League baseball team. An avid writer and sports enthusiast, he has authored 16 additional books on sports topics. In his downtime Peter enjoys family time with his wife and two young children and attending hockey and baseball games in his home city.